ZION ROSES

Zion Roses, with its alluring title, builds impressively on the promise of Minott's *Kumina Queen*. The pursuit of self-realisation runs through interrelated themes such as family, ancestors, the challenges of a girl's growing into womanhood, and these grounded in the history of African-Jamaican slave experience. She engraves Jamaican folk culture in her wordscape, as in the sequence that revives 'jonkonnu', the theatre of the streets. Art and music become integral parts of the experience, as in the poems about Jean-Michel Basquiat, Paul Gauguin and trombonists Don Drummond and Rico Rodriguez. The title poem, which closes the collection, is a song of praise, instinct, in the nuances of the title itself, with the issues explored in the preceding range of poems. The Zion of Christianity interplays with Rastafarian, and 'Roses' illuminates each.

— Edward Baugh

In *Zion Roses* the voices that people Minott's poetry share histories of loss and acts of defiance. From poem to poem we are in the presence of a different story-teller, captivating us with what they have witnessed and what they know. Minott's imagination travels and through seemingly effortless tonal shifts we are in the company of 'Bag-a-Wire – an Endangered Soul', of Telemachus ('original rasta and broom seller'), of unnamed ancestors of those displaced by the middle passage, and, in a sequence of brilliantly restless renditions, the painter and radical Jean-Michel Basquiat. Weaving in and out and letting everybody speak, we hear the poet herself reporting on injustice and hope. Minott tells histories of colonialism. She shares what it means to love. And in a series of profound meditations she articulates faith. *Zion Roses* is the work of a generous and gifted poet, 'eloquent at the green of daybreak'.

— David Herd

'I see visions wider than all the nets cast' ends one of the poems. Winsome also hears said visions; so much cultural lustre and light is "languaged" here, a strong song that is mythic as it is rapturously melodic. The poems are no mere voiceovers but lyrics inflected with the sight of history. These poer   'ed and dignified living.

T0164046

ackson

ALSO BY MONICA MINOTT

Kumina Queen

ZION ROSES

MONICA MINOTT

PEEPAL TREE

First published in Great Britain in 2021
Peepal Tree Press Ltd
17 King's Avenue
Leeds LS6 1QS
UK

ISBN 13: 9781845235178

Supported using public funding by
ARTS COUNCIL
ENGLAND

CONTENTS

BAG-A WIRE – AN ENDANGERED SOUL

We arrive, anywhere we land, landless,
refugees of a kind, like goats on Redonda
arriving on sinking ships, yet claiming space,
pondering nationalism and spatial dissonance,
till we meet Bag-a-Wire on rhythm. Survivor.

Bag-a-Wire is chief suspect, though no one's sure
what he's guilty of, not yet. Shaking shoulders
move in opposition to his feet. Since the 1907
earthquake, survivors tek time walking round,
always expecting a shifting of ground, sky and

food shortage. Children learn conservation,
suspicion of food & safety behind zinc fences,
to frown on registration numbers/identity cards,
especially when as a teenager Bagga try scuffle
likkle food after hurricane Charlie breeze-blow.

Director call security, security come. "A wha you do
bwoy, thief free food?" Strung him to a light post,
"You go pay fe thief boy." Slapped with cutlass,
blade to neck, Bagga hollered; they left him for dead.
He listens for rattling sounds – souls of men hiding.

He knows deprivation, exiled by the exiled. He has
hope, not that of hospitable men who die in bed
asphyxiated by the fumes of poets reading verse
fed by liquorish fires of hopelessness. He keeps pressing
in spite of wire fences, and bad-mindedness.

Nowhere to stay, dressed for three days, on red alert
for a place called Dignity. Danger resides in this
confession, an acknowledgement of loss, and loss
yet to be defined. Bundled into exile, we cease
worrying about changelings, we walk with Angels

while halting tongues take pause. "Is better to
starve and dead," Bagga say, "than compromise."
Angels allow him to take mental photographs
of people and places to which he'll never return.
Exile, a rake, muting Redonda.

UNDOCUMENTED

Men, women and children were game.
The exact number of Congolese hands
severed, undocumented.

Leopold II sparked the trade, rubbery hands
in need of civilization, cuffed, cut off.
Unmapped jungle-hands

strung-up overhead, crackling like fire,
smoked free from dark bodies. Unmarked,
yet free in the dark continent.

Missionary Sheppard counted 81 free hands
at one sitting; those who came up short
on delivery received this kingly gift:

hands separated from wrists. Leo's greatest
life skill. Who dared argue death's offering
in the Congo Free State?

Brown pigmented chocolate, epigenetic scars,
flashbacks now cut-off my breath, triggering
the new *Great Forgetting*.

TROMBONE BLUES

i: *Don's Perspective*

It would not be unthinkable
the jazz, the Sirens in his soul
like bag-a-wire blues driving
sailors to shipwreck, to forget
the music of home.

Imagination stripped him bare
on the edge of Torrington bridge.
He blew his matchless horn, hard. No one
cared, as he looked over at intractable death,
and said to himself, "A lover can bear only so much sadness."
Peisinoe wailed once more. Walking home, he chose death.

ii: *Margarita Speaks*

The first day she heard sirens wail,
Margarita asked, "Did he undress me
one last time without my knowing? He
wanting to possess me, keep me from
dancing rhumba, but rhumba is who I am.

He settled on plan B, what death proposes –
a short absence, skin losing colour,
heat disappearing, under thin flowers
of misunderstandings, toppling rhumba.

All I want is love, but love is hard to remember
I settle for unspeakable sadness, wanting
to lock horns, yet skip strangulation.

I feel his touch again, the nightmare renders
me speechless; last air leaving my body
makes him dumb."

iii: *A Brush With Death*

She was just a thought, a shape,
a body, an everythingness, now
a truth like death. "Margarita, please!"
he cried as his city grew old, his lover
put on a new face, and he walked
steadfast with his loss to a police post
crying out, "Margarita – gone."

WHEN TO LEAVE THE SHALLOWS

By faith I rise from the bed of shallows.
I have fished all night, and caught five parrot-fish –
which I ought to toss back to clean the reefs. And here
he comes again in the startling morning light, with no
apology, telling me to toss my net once more into the deep;
his horizon smile, his encompassing ageless arms
beckon and I am stunned by my own reflection,
a new gleam like magic portraits my features. I step out
leaving the desolation I have made for myself; shambles
of last evening's starless night silence any protest left
in me; I gaze steadfastly at the light on the sea,
I see visions wider than all the nets cast,
as I set out to walk on water.

ME, MAHOGANY TREE, NOW TOUR GUIDE

He stood six feet tall, strong-wide shoulders, skin cool to the touch,
black as charcoal, chiselled cheekbones, Koromante legs. He lifted
his hands to the hills, pointing to Cockpit country, "As far as you can
see is part of a plantation named 'Good Hope'. The Plantation is
history and sepulchre holding bones and rattling chains of slavery.
Who better to be a tourist guide (thousands of lives sacrificed at the
altar of sugar) than the great grandson of a slave?"

Tall
    wide shoulders
        Koromante legs.

Hills
    Cockpit country
        Good Hope.

Plantation
    history
        in ruins.

Bones
    rattling
        altar of slaves.

Crows circling miles of banana plants laden
with fruit; he smiled as he mentioned the
Good Hope Great House. "Look, the garage,
former slave quarters. Crowning gift of land."
His gaze levelled green plantain suckers.

Great grandmother
        was land, yet not land.
            Colonel & friends guilty

of rape, yet not rape.
                    The plantation guilty
                              not guilty of arduous service.

Colonel, officer and fiend, maker of history.
After each rape a woman went out, picked limes,
sucked and washed herself with lime juice.
No time for artifacts: bracelets, ankle-cuffs.

The guide paused
                    a mahogany tree
                              scarred trunk

bloodied backs
                    generational markers
                              history and sepulchre.

Turning his back to his guests the guide
removed his shirt. "Imagine," he said.

ii)

"Imagine a mahogany tree complicit in
the sins of the man people called Massa.
After each beating the pain travelling down
into the roots became tight knots. The tree
longing for rainwater to seep in, to carry
life-nutrients to kill the festering growth.
Often the tree told stories to wild birds
seeking refuge in its branches. Refugees.
They understood the life of roaming,
wild birds carrying today's news.

iii)

"People 'fraid walk through plantation
at night. They swear they hear *jumbie*
rumblings, although the grave quieten
him some, but not enough for the likes of
Rema, Pam and all them gals' mamas
him did like fe touch." The guide senses
movement among visitors as they
huddle close, sisters hugging sisters,
black men holding their women tight,
real tight, white tourists' poker faces
wet, as we turn to exit Good Hope.

PASSOVER

You must have read Morris's take on Pilate,
how he washed "histrionic hands" before
he nailed Him, before he sat down to eat.
But it was the scribes (you and I) that set
it up, wrote of blasphemy; is so we always
get in a mix-up, always have something
to say. Lonely artists scratching for trouble
back-up in a coloured Jesus – fi we Saviour.

"How I so sure about that?" His face
shone brighter than money; something
to write about. Truth is truth; Judas's crosses
carry him into the field of blood; "Glad we had
no hand in that." See, grave birds hovering:
Is a dose of conscience kill him. Feet dangling,
no shoes on his feet, no staff in his hand.
No sojourner to share in the Passover.

SPIRITS

Don't bring no ghost in my front door – Bessie Smith

It was the day I arrived,
Father blew the abeng
long and hard; the sound carried.
I looked around and decided
I had some growing to do,
and fast, if I was to keep up.
Mama said I sat up at four months,
walked at seven, talked at nine,
but father shook his head, said,
"Slow down girl, no need to rush."
Soon I was sixteen. I still can hear his voice:
"Boys just looking to bruck their ducks,
they don't even know how to pull up
their drawers, yet they out there trying
to score; don't know how ole people travel
from Africa, the bodies they saw tossed, the
fire into which brothers jumped, don't know
that the sky is old; youth only thinking
'bout cock-crow, and nice-time.
Maybe they are the ones travelling, spirits
that never had the time to say prayers."

WHY TELEMACHUS SELLS BROOM

And I is Telemachus,
original rasta and broom seller.
After the big man
dust out the rascal crew
stalking the house like jackals,
I and I had to flee
to Bobo Hill for fortification.

I imagined I-self as
Odysseus, with bushy locks
hanging like petals, blooms
from a poor man orchid.
Was not hard to engraft
I-self, an learn 'bout Niyabinghi
and Twelve Tribes of Israel.

But the I became confused,
which I was the right I?
Must a Black man have a
Black God, and sell broom
to reach heaven? And if
worse come to the worse,
should I, Telemachus,
cut mi locks and fly?

BETTER STRANGERS

In the cool of evening growing into night,
I listen to Beres' tunes. I forget time while reliving walks
along this hillside where Grandma's house once stood.
I hum choruses. I know everything there is to know
about nursing, curing ailments, giving back and belly rubs,
sousing down and dem other things that ease the heart,
mek man feel like him born to win. Suddenly, I am aware
of a shadow over my left shoulder searching for company.
I smile that quirky smile; I have been here before, sitting at this
same table, drinking my favourite martini, looking out as waves
toss. *The sea is unsteady tonight.* A steady drizzle adds a chill
to an evening begging for closeness. I look to the sky, I nod
to his request: *Hope we can become better strangers.* I sense in
him a certainty bolstered by smooth black skin, and chiselled
cheekbones. If he was a mannequin, I'd trust myself
to first measure his sure feet and not his lion eyes; I'd fashion a
gold bracelet as his only cover, a picture-perfect photograph
set against a night sea, for us to acknowledge God and creation.
Next, I'd look for wounds, dark patches of hurt, marking many
battles. The smoke from the food-fire seasons air;
passersby seem not to be bothered by earth tremors.

What I am not sure of, I know I'll find in his rhythmic pulse
as we define intensity by reflex, translate touch into feeling,
bring healing to unnourished passive cells, restore vigour.
I watch for light-out, the glow of dusk streaking highlights on
our nakedness, his taut biceps and triceps as he casually lifts me
and fits himself steady between ready legs. Saturday evening,
the bustling street traffic has no time to contemplate what may
be happening between man and woman in an abandoned cove
twenty meters below the road, and a stone's throw from
an argumentative sea. A slow rising moon enters a red sky
while buyers and sellers haggle over closing sales: yam
bananas and tomatoes, cheap; another sound-system-man

strings his wire on the public service line, a coconut vendor
shaves the last three jellies left on his stall. *Coconut water
good to quiet thirst, and wash clean the heart.* Tonight my
heart is clean and full. I have left writings on his thigh, marking
melodies of Beres' music, signalling the stage of the hunt.

Waves send water tumbling into our cave, as the tides inch
in little by little; we are knee deep in water, only then do we climb
to higher ground, to a rock flattened by constant motion of the sea.
The night has come alive, party people arrive as we slip into dripping
garments. We walk boldly to First Street as if we were the only people
in town, windblown shirt, skirt, and pants almost dry. We ignore
quizzical glances and frowns, knowing that the soft paws of passion,
trailing an illuminating light, made us better than strangers,
made us wild and beautiful beings.

UNDER A DARKER SUN

In every town centre they planted a clock,
a mark that civilization had come, that the enslaved
no longer depended on the sun. Two hundred years
later we still in revolt. All fourteen clocks now silent.

Massa Tom build house next door to a raging river,
within a mile of river mouth. The river emptied into
a stormy sea, losing itself. Each morning he'd wait out
the clock's fifth gong, before recognising morning,

before he left his bed of cotton and myrrh, brushing the
bruised body of one of us girls he had selected to ride.
I remember the night he selected me; maybe my agile limbs,
ready smile showing white, white teeth had attracted him.

The clock stuck nine; he pulled me from mother's bed.
I was only thirteen. My black smooth skin wrinkled under
his gaze. White rum sour on his breath, he pulled me close,
"You will be all right, soon you will be wanting it," he said.

Growing up, I had overheard whispered stories of men
mounting girls, before melting into rain-washed skin.
Like an arrow unleashed into the heart of a young warrior,
an unprovoked smell of rain-soaked earth assailed me.

As he entered me, I shuddered. Stone upon stone.
Surely I would suffocate, would die. Cold upon coal,
a searching hand found my land, ripped a thin veil
before a disarticulated body surrendered. I fainted.

Early morning bell sounded one, two, three, four,
I saw him naked atop bloodstained bed.
I knew I could kill him, knew I should kill him, but
gathered my flourbag frock, under a darker sun.

WHAT NOT TO REGRET

I try not to regret myself,
the tipping force of memory,
of will, of nature, of a woman
who knows with concrete certainty
what she wants, not burdened
by coincidences of wanting. So
not to betray myself, I turn, seeking
someone to blame, and there
she is un-moveable, Mama Ignota.
No-one chose her, her name means
the forgotten one, survivor of pit toilets,
miscarriages, near rapes, a father lost at sea.
She never accepted no, when it should be yes.
There is something to be said about
epic genetic markers, about sisters who
bungie-jump, smouldering tightrope walkers
with no safety nets. Now my sixteen-year-old
daughter declares her desired profession:
to pilot planes into volcanic-erupting
mountains to measure heat intensity.

My mama raised chance daughters
marrying truth with chance, and here
I am trying to regret truth, but can't.

SET SAIL

(*for V.S. Naipaul*)

I looked up to grey English skies and felt absent.
No poui tree, no poinciana, no river of golden dust.
I am in the land of my captors, those who took
my tongue and gave me English. I find myself musing
in unknown tongues, not sure of my utterances, but it
feel right. I pick up a book in my longing for home,
V.S. Naipaul's *The Middle Passage*. He talk bout fools
who rejected federation, *yam and breadfruit niggers* on deck.
What am I guilty of? Seh they running from cut-'gainst and
boil-down, sailing for equal to equal respect. They bigger fools
than even I. But I too am tired, tired of failure masked by
calypso's virtues and indifference, by the absence of history,
and the pitching of tents, like we occupying camp site. I am
walking down Oxford Street and I think of my friend, Mushay;
he never left Trinidad. The last thing I heard, he had a tumour
growing in his gut, inoperable. He was the true carnival-loving
Trini, never missed an opportunity to party. But here I am, finding
fault with everything, now wondering if I made the right
decision to come here where the sky's always grey.
I feel hemmed in, I bawl out to the all-knowing God
who said, "Keep sailing... No impurities in running water."

PENNY KILL SHILLING

De man no dead but slavemaster bury him.
No matter how him holler, "Massa, me no dead yet,"
Massa answer, "Carry him go 'long."
What do we call that? Some call it profit.
Some call it wickedness.

I am the last in the line of the man Massa bury.
My great-grandmother run to the hills
same day, with Papa in she belly. Papa
was a wild one, kill plenty backra. Each time
he kill one him say, "Massa me no dead yet."

Now we sing ole song and tell ole stories;
we remember white man named Dunbar
who act as spy for Maroons, tek him mek warning,
all who come for 'Science', never double spy.
Maroon tek action. Penny kill shilling.

DUNBAR CREEK TO NIGERIA
TWO HUNDRED YEARS LATER.

The water spirit brought us here
far from the shores of Africa.
The water spirit will take us back,
seventy-five Igbos, chains rattling,
on our way back home.

WHEN LOSS IS GAIN

Joy is not something we women manufacture.
Trials was nothing new to great-granny,

nana, auntie, nor sista – all ubiquitous queens.
When trouble tumble down like thunderstorm

we tremble, "set big-tent defence", batten down
as sorrows creep, fierce, unshakable, on target.

It hard to understand how Blossom face bright
and smiling when she get the cussing of her life

last night from her wutliss, drunk-a-ready husband
Joe, but she dry her tears in secret, wash sorrows

in a baptismal cloth, and lift a song, *Praise Ye*
from whom all blessings flow. Is as if the music

spin Blossom from hearing Joe's swearing: "I sorry
the day a put ring pon that deh finger, plenty high-

colour gal did waan me, look how you black an...
Could be me did drink mad-pus-piss an mad."

The more him cuss, the more Blossom sing, *Praise*
him all creatures here below. At times she squeeze

foot-a-ground to keep from tek the nearest dutchy
and clobber him head, but she know by morning

Joe is a different Joe, no memory of hard words.
He said, "I born come see mother and her mother

lifting songs of praise," believing Caribbean people
must count not what was lost, *for every loss is gain*,

though we witness how cousin Warrick tek time meagre
down; neither bath nor oil could save him. Faith is what

him lack. Faith is what Mama and Aunt Merci have
in abundance. Yet, Mama ask God, "Why me unlucky so?"

Mama tell me how she work hard, open haberdashery.
Six months later hurricane Charlie blow the roof to sky.

Everything was lost. But she knew the lesson, *Every loss
is gain*. Mama cry her cry, wipe her tears in frock-tail,

brush her hair, and go out to find love-of-self in
a job again. Who to decide whether geographic loss

is greater loss than remaining in born-place, for
trouble come, when and to whom it will.

So to tek pain out of serious things, we who know better
teach youth to overcome, for we know *every loss is gain*.

FLOORBOARDS – ORACABESSA

Jagged rocks and the crashing sea mock fond
memories of Oracabessa – a two hour journey swollen
into four punishing hours, children padded with news-
paper on our chests to cut the need for vomit stops.
By the time we arrived at Annotto Bay, a brisk breeze
and a blue-green sea brought relief, resettling beliefs.
My stomach lurched, my heart smiled, hopeful some
good could come of the journey into Mother's land.

Arriving at a four-foot, cut-stone fence, a space for a gate,
a tiny two-bedroom house with lattice windows trimmed
with purple vines, set some distance from the road, a reward
for weary travellers. Not sure how many sisters came on the trip.
Yet, I remember as children we rushed to the front door,
pausing on each step to examine the brilliant red floorboards,
making my smile shine, willing me to examine cracks and
missing pieces, highlighting frosted window panes.

Crashing waves jar me to the present; floorboards
temporarily forgotten, I listen to rhythmic heave and throw
of the waves as I walk from room to room. Kitchen,
dining and an open living room had not been swallowed up
by the persistent hammering of waves. All remain intact. Gaps
in the floorboards randomly patterned, expected. Treasures
hidden in a cellar below: coins, pencils, rings, rock-piercing
heartaches, hard-pressed by time, alive just below surface.

DAD NAMED HER GENEVIEVE

He knew she'd be magnificent.
Her name in French is defender,
always interrupting avenues of lack
with morning eruptions.
Imagine her six-foot tall, a woman who
takes the fight to tumultuous fears,
and the earth is better for the fight
that left her hair white with wonder.
Imagine her black gums brighter than
the flash of a camera. Imagine her scent
trailing wayward winds, seducing storms.
See where she moves; she leaves healing.
She lost a grandson, buried a husband, yet
no tears will bleed away God's blessings,
no miracle sighting, no crying statue, no
certification. *Her children rise and call her
blessed.* Daughter of Arthur and Ignota,
she'll never be like those who slipped out
of their names. Sister to overcoming days,
glisten like unbroken glass; years of planting
seeds leave no time for regret.

BEFORE THE RAINS CAME

The day she started talking to herself
I was nine or so; it was like a drizzle.

It became a habit, till she'd shout back
at the thunder; for hours she wept unceasingly.

Winds became stronger. All that time I'd
creep around apprehensive, not knowing

whether she heard me. I learned
not to be afraid of the flood of tears.

What would you do if you were me? she asked.
I had no answer at ten or at thirteen; at fifteen

she stopped crying. She sat in a chair and rocked.
I called, "Mama, Mama." No answer.

There would be no answer in her silence
in the drought-stricken weeks that followed.

We got up, made breakfast, washed dishes.
Dad went to work. Hundreds of rainflies

attracted to a glowing yellow light,
came each night before the rains.

RUNDOWN

Mama took the kitchen cloth
and dabbed her eyes, hoping
none of her children would see.
Peeling the yellow yam,
Mama know when starch dry
it go well with the rundown
simmering in the dutch pot.

Outside the kitchen window
boys play marbles, girls pretend
to be mamas on tippy toes.
A smile opens her memory.
She once played dress-up, swishing
bony hips down an imaginary catwalk,
and where did it get her? Over a stove
watching the persistent tide pull back
much of what it had promised.

Mama watch cracks in earth
swallow jazz shoes, as brush strokes
fade, while rotting husks of coconut
drift out to sea, each husk a log entry
recording a would-be landfall.

She shut her eyes tight, desperate
to stem the gathering flow of tears;
kneading dumplings into compliance,
peeling and trimming knots in yam,
dicing potatoes, grating coconuts,
weeping again into our next meal.

A SKYPE VISIT WITH KEISHA AS SHE WALKS
KARTEL INTO AN AURORA
(for Keisha, a soldier on base in the US army, 2016)

A black rose pulled by both sea and sky, her steps
parallel to the horizon on a wayward beach.
It is eleven-thirty pm in Jamaica, and six-thirty pm
in Hawaii as we walk Kartel on this stony patch.

Keisha's neighbour, who is walking her dog,
asks through a shifty smile, "Are you waiting for
the green?" *Funny question!* Shielded from the
buzz of smart phones and ear buds, she can't

hear me, unintentional eavesdropper. Yet, I raise
my eyes, tracking her pointed line of vision where
sea meets sky. Sure now that I am hallucinating,
a God-green glow appears, a quickening flare-up,

a geomagnetic storm ringing circles in my head.
What might be is not what is. In Venus' orbit I'm
surrounded by shouts of sunflowers; I hear unborn
children, picnic-ready lovers say, "You are lovely."

I hesitate to speak inauthentic words. Keisha
stands still; paradise would have none of us.
We watch the green slowly take shape;
perspiration unfolds me, daylight gives

its best to night. Strays avoid soldiers.
Suffused in the hope of a setting green,
I flutter like a bird wanting to be free,
toss like a worrisome, heaving sea. Under

a haze ten sea-grape trees line the shore,
as green continues to pour from the sky,
till my sky-canvas' colour is complete. Then
we are safe, Kartel, a soldiering Keisha, and I.

STILTS

i:
Grandma Ethel was blameless.
Conscience clean of shadows,
knew the time between dusk and
night when soldier crabs roamed.

Under her house on stilts
the sea roared miles below
as urchins gathered. Reflections,
none wanting salvation.

ii:
I dive into a rock-formed pool,
rocks that had Ethel pondering
as she watched passing ships put
out to sea. I feel unsettled.

A new entrant sends waves
in spasms from the ocean floor.
Ethel believed in such a promise,
midday fire on skin. His hands.
It was his hands that drove stilts
into rocks this hard? Rocks having
endured battering for centuries,
as sea birds catch their bearings.
Blue skies wearing flowery dresses,
talc-fresh skin meets the sea. Man
overboard: *Drop anchor.* It was
then she saw ash on her feet.

A sailor dives, his skin glistening,
he surfaces a touch away, eyes
watching what he wants; fortune
betrays him, he accepts his loss.

iii:
An interloper climbed the stilts
entering our domain. Crab soup,
a crafty handiwork. Crack the claws.
She prays that memory is eternal.

Suitcases packed, passport ready,
leaving behind the house on stilts.
Daybreak images: scent of honey,
freshly-baked bread, crab cakes.
No sand to fashion graves.
No moon on Madison Avenue, no
beanstalk to climb, just enough room
to mourn his childhood days

before New York had meaning,
hippie-power and shared love.
Now pleurisy held his breath;
Ethel held a telegram. "Come

quick, Cecil too weak to fight."
Ethel returned to a grieving sea,
three children soldiering on as if
the gatecrasher had not entered.

iv:
A lemon-drop martini in hand,
I speak to the ghosts of Ethel and
Cecil, to crabs inhabiting shadows
commanding them to memorize

scriptures: I am the messenger
of hope. A cormorant dives,
an octopus lashes out; together
we become like a new gospel.

WHEN LOVE LEAVES

Perhaps that boy who went to his father
for new shoes, who fidgeted for hours, waiting,
who sat ready to catch a passing love, moving
in its own way like wind-blown August rain,
perhaps, if his father had not sneaked away,
had not left him there till darkness came,
he would have proposed more than a torrid
affair, wet and wild and full of longing. Now
he says that his answer should have been
more than a walk on a summer evening,
more than picking bissy to purge his blood,
more than an incomplete sentence, stranded
among paragraphs of deaf commitments.
Now he says he is ready to face a gaping
wound, early childhood tremblings.
"I am a boy again, inching myself off a stool,
gingerly placing my feet on the ground,
shoe-bottom flapping, walking towards home
and Mama's bitter cerasee that had no cure
for when love leaves."

LET US PLAY BY MY RULES

I have been called, yes called
to a city where boys grow into skeletons
and skulls, wearing halos of nails and thorns,
where locusts deconstruct and strip-down,
like I strip down for you, show you my lines,
my angles, my crown. They cross over me,
Madonna, to feel what black-crazy feels like.
They cross me over, sit me down, sing me
soft, sing me wild, ring me with fire. Then
they listen when I testify, a broken heart,
loud, back-talking loud, before they reply,
calling out my name, Jean Michel Basquiat.
I say, "Off with their grinning heads."

THE RADIANT CHILD

(In the after-life Jean-Michel Basquiat talks of loneliness)

i:
I guess lonely has no mama
he goes searching for stories like me
to cling to, to make his sovereignty whole.

ii:
But don't give me that same old shit,
don't want it no more; rather surrender this
black scrawny body, rather sprout wings.

I sing my alone God songs in e-flat
colour where I walk, colour as I see fit.
No same ole, same ole, I'm tired of it!

Why are my lines spiderweb thin
on which I balance reality, and where
will this road, my road, your road end?

iii: *Jean-Michel Basquiat reviews death through the eyes of a few friends*

Kelle, my girl talked of me with tears in her eyes.
"He said he was clean; no red or blue capsules,
I tried reaching him; no answer. But he had me."

"The last time I saw him on a bar stool, alone,"
Baghoomian remembered, young black artist,
"on my last new year's eve night."

"He returned to New York City in the summer of '88.
New York is so fucked up and lonely in summer,"
another scribbling artist recalled my return.

No mistake, my finding life and death as twins;
genius, mixed-up gene codes tagged madness,
and I ask myself, "What's the best age for dying?"

While they were contemplating closeness to fame, I
am on my pilgrimage to prophesy; #27, the final number.
I paint, and paint myself radiant, into black light.

Oh black light I follow you, oh black light I follow you.
It was as if my brush knew the way, for it carried me
a far way into my journey, before it said goodbye.

SCRIBBLINGS
for Jean-Michel Basquiat

You want to rob spray-painted crowns?
Again? You can't take my crown.

You want to understand my scribblings,
undream my post-living reality?

I understand the rake; you wanting
what is not mine to give. Rakes.

Not even I understand a dung heap.
I set it on fire. Smoke. Riverton dump.

Dropped school or school dropped me
It figures why I scribble and scribble.

Expelled from the womb into death,
A crowning of life. Ashes to ashes.

I light fires in my forest, I watch them
burn bright. Scythe or sickle ready.

Iron cool, iron medium-hot. A hoe
in the forest, not a metaphoric hoe,

a hoe to dig deep, plant corn. Corn
not gunshot, not GM corn. Real corn.

Harvest. Workers with spray guns,
witnessing corn crushed at their feet.

Vanishing line of graffiti artists, we paint,
we scribble. Messengers of woe.

ANTIDOTE

(Jean-Michel Basquiat's writes)

Take my crown if you will,
I've decided to drop out
of this secret society,
not so secret anymore.
Anyone can spray-paint
public walls, not just me.
The last living saint
split the scene, spikes
piercing his forehead.

Lose that ego, fuck worry;
the antidote of life is death,
easy – always in reach. Inhale,
hold a breath: one, two, three.
Feel the air lift you high high;
I work best naked. I undress
into perfection. Teach cunning
above sad-self; agile last breath
works its way, running from
extremity to extremity, to glory.

A BEAUTIFUL CORPSE
(Jean-Michel Basquiat 1961-1988)

The art dealers lined up.
Yes, he was indeed beautiful. Yet
they left before we buried his body.
His going had no code, body laid out.
It was time for the counting:
the rains came.

I got a hole in my soul
I heard Jean say, *a hole*
so large, only death can
fill it. I got a hole in my
pocket, I heard the answer,
Just one more painting
before you go.

METAL MAN VS BIRD ON MONEY

After Jean-Michel Basquiat's Metal Man vs Bird On Money

What is left of him?
The Bird on money
sunken eyes spitting
stones; over-arching
ear to ear connectivity,
an electromagnetic pull,
disjointed limbs weighing
in the balance. A heavy
heart pondering reasonings,
profit or no profit. Prophet.
Lightning strikes the tree
illuminating spines; silver
horizontal smoke currents run
amok, disrupt the system
set. Look for shadows:
haughty men and dreamers
arrive at the wrong time.
Nothing but heavy metal.
Metal man helping to rake
in profit. Bird swallows metal.
Neck-back, money bird dead.
Armageddon.

SELF PORTRAIT AS A HEEL

After Jean Michel Basquiat's painting with the same name.

A version of my story: "He stepped
out, heel first, breach." The first woman
superimposing thoughts on me since
I left, and look at where she chose to
start, me, Basquiat, as a heel. A laugh.

I am laughing. Here is poetic justice.
I could do worse; it could have been
Basquiat as a slippery eel, or Basquiat
as a finger-sucking matchstick man.

I examine man's transgressions, stuck at
lesson 1: no Black heroes in Hollywood.
I have been gone some twenty years but
little has changed. A mulatto trumpeter

walks in. His name is Jazz. "Play me," I
dare him. Soon he is relegated to be me,
plays a small part in a skit… kills himself.
Did someone say *the recurring heel*?

What a nice boy. Why did he do it?
He made good tackling the status quo.
No guarantees for a well-heeled graffiti
artist. It was then it came to me, or

she spoke to me, saying, "Make an
appeal for every wronged man that
went the way you did. Untimely.
Do you mourn loss of love or loss?"

I don't think so. It was the pain, drugs,
and wood chips falling like rain. I search
now as I searched then for cover. None.
A shrill sound hammering my brain.

I need to get rid of rage. I heard "Run!"
So I ran. I left room for them to mourn.
Today I rock back on my heels, I feel a
surge. Equilibrium? I lose balance again.

MALEVICH AND I

(For Kazimir Severinovich Malevich, 1879 –1935)

He painted me in secret, a changing abstraction.
I am no more, no less than the first Black Square.
He hid me for months, kept me close to his touch,
not wanting to share an abandonment with
a world not ready to receive me, as he had.
And he, my lover, realised while rediscovering
cosmic patterns, moving geometry up a notch,
art needed none of it. No, not the first Black
Square, the second, nor even a Red Square.
Art needed no one, it never did.

DEGAS COMING OF AGE –
HIS FINAL WORK STILL TO COME

i:
Perhaps if Degas could, he'd paint
a ballet skirt of fire, consuming
copper legs, burning into shape
Carib and Maroon together.

ii:
You'll find me in monotypes,
what you can see of me, skirt
and feet yet to be reformed,
pink ballet shoes, arms in fifth;
one or two phantoms following

as if they are spin-off dancers,
as if we had one soul, tainted
by light and sorrow. Violated
mid-air, working for throwaway
shoes, we brag at our ruination,

worry that our soles will not
be better. We become creatures
of his voyeur creation, faceless.
He extracts light out of a muted past,
spins us on tippy toes. Desperate,

we make it out of dying skirts,
hair ablaze, synchronized fire
tipping the balance, the grip
of night tightening, as we slip
away to empty dressing rooms.

COMPARING CHAMBERS
Working with Vincent Van Gogh

My chamber is much like the one he painted,
a basic wooden bed set against a wooden floor,
two circumspect aged chairs, trimmed in gold
rather than *yellow fresh butter* (we are not
expecting many guests), two photographs
of dear loved ones on the near wall, while
other pictures of places travelled, scattered
pastel colours, drift into nooks and crannies
in no special order. No blue water goblet,
no matching wash pan; the brown door
answers to brown French windows, not
green; throw-cushions and blankets are
chalky red, though I'd rather not talk colour,
but of the sensuous softness of wool when
pressed against my skin and, by way of balance,
books he left unread, books:
bright lamps to light away dark hours.

OUT OF ACES

The Joker – Carnival of Grotesques
Ensor, 1892

I found the joker living in the Old Masters' museum
captured by Ensor as he captivated his subjects;
sitting with no pretext, the joker cannot hide.

A pack of cards on display: the Queen
of Hearts, a long-lost friend, had thrown a fit,
her four kings – nowhere to be found.

Perhaps my king got lost in the bush,
under a local moon full of misgivings.
It is said only an ace can lure them back.

I am out of aces. The joker, a stand-up man,
sits squarely on top of the stacked pack.
He's the character in real life dramas,

dressing the part, garishly painted from head
to toe, a page-turner in Gotham & comic books,
made to take the rap for the bizarre follies

everyday people commit.
"Victor, quack or foe?" a question to ask.
"Who would gladly play his part?"

LOOK… THERE ARE MANSIONS HERE
(Tribute to Cleveland 'Mac' Johnson)

It was a thought far removed from his mind;
auspicious Death would drop by on a leisurely
afternoon, more like an unexpected friend.
And wasn't Death surprised by his welcome,
so accustomed to men hiding and plotting,
wanting to extend their stay? Here was a soldier
ready for battle, a sailor ready for breaking waves.
As the second wind lifted, April leaves quivered,
his faith held; he tilted his head and smiled.

It was a thought removed from his mind
that there would be a crack or break from light,
for light can only be light. Yet, some among us
would question his absence, wondering why
twisting, winding winds gallop into eternity.
A hammering certainty defied death, headless
fear, wilted and worn, vanished. As death lost
its sting, he tilted his head and smiled.
"Look there are mansions here," he cried.

RAE TOWN ROCK
(for Rico Rodriquez, 1934-2015)

A devotee of the music you play,
the shuffle, the riff
caught me down Salt Lane.
A little scurrying here,
a little scuffling there,
you blow your trombone; glad
fishermen throw their nets
into the blue; landing a shoal of
blue-note parrot fish, open mouths
receiving rhythms. The rock and
the steady brought tears to my eyes,
sent me in search of the womb of
deep waters, imaginations shaped,
birthing enough to feed me. The
music is sowing and reaping,
the music has silver wings.

THE OTHER LEFT FOOT PLEASE

(For the late Barry Moncrieffe)

I had no tutu years, I had Uncle Barry instead.
We met weekday evenings at six for movement.
Pull on leotards, tighten tummy muscles, push-up
sprouting breasts before strutting our way to class.
We danced for the love of it.

Anchor years, rehearsing steps, following majestic lines,
off moves became camera-ready, polished, supple,
ready for exploration. It is true what they say of dancers:
trained rib muscles, tight, projecting speech and laughter
into fingers and toes, pulsing versed instruments

as musicians would a horn or a fife, a knowing
light appearing in us, same light provoking all-nighters,
dancing, moving till morning comes – always too soon.
Monday evenings, a seemingly startled Uncle B would say,
"And you who keep eating too much rice and peas,

come wanting me to create summer bodies? No
miracles here today. On the floor, on your backs,
fifty leg raises" – we all versed in that move –
"on each side fifty more. Corner.
Second position, cross the floor,
lead with the right; and you ladies with two left
feet, please repeat the exercise." Poor
Gloria, she never could get it right, but
never would give up. Respect due, Ms. G.

Departures came. Homo, our best dancer
(that is how he introduced himself –
late seventies a different time),
wore the jazziest green nail polish the day
he announced, "I am leaving the rock.
Off to New York City."

News came, he'd died. So quickly! We did not
live the brittleness of death with him, but
cried, accepted, moved on.
Sick and bleeding days followed.
When a dancer missed rehearsals for
more than a few classes, panic and tears
washed the dance floor.
Duran's squat features duped many,
his testimony, flight mid-air, before
landing soft as a bird.
Duran once pointed to runs
in my tights while choreographing a dance.
Musing, I relive every lift, each turn,
split, lock step in that moment.
I still hear the words of the song
making us both want to fly…
"I want to hold you till I die."
Duran died the following year.

I visit Uncle B now and then,
squeeze his hands; he is mostly okay.
Phantom dancers have vanished,
a fierce love present. He would not speak
of bad luck, nor do we count our dead.

BECAUSE DEATH HAS NO FORM

I impress my therapist,
I explore form.
I write about Mandy;
our paths crossed once.
She is also a writer,
but I see her pallid skin,
thin cheeks, face still
as a photograph,
a death-haunting stare
willing the room silent.
In a measured voice
Mandy declares,
"Death won't hurt me, I
can die without a sound."
I look deep in her throat,
see her as she wants to
be seen. I close my eyes,
see her then, dressed in
her always black slacks,
writing her perfect line.

THE SEA WILL CLAIM US ALL

(for Grandfather Cecil Campbell)

Stones tossed from another shore,
we rewrite our language into Creole.
Who hears tragedy in oceans, in shells,
in sand, when our feet become fins?

We leave exposed cracks in contours
of a continent; in the eclipse of Africa,
colour-stains rain from wounded reefs.
We get here, cure-all salt of the earth,

travelling free like tragedy. I am but one
fragment, washed-up on an eastern shore.
Yet you sail west to find something of me;
of Columbus & "horned monsters". I dream

a kinked soul, epicentre of an ocean's
quarrels. It's no longer about Odysseus
and shipwrecks – he has done his time
on earth. Earth guts and drowns old fish

and sailors. I mourn a grandfather.
I follow a moving finger's trajectory,
a rising of mad blackbirds. My brother
flashes crazy-mean locks at the sky.

I'm with him in a landlocked cove,
in the haze of smoke from a man-spliff
shuttling against the old secret
of the sea's selection: man overboard – his name

Cecil. The humming of the ocean makes
you sick; the drag of water heavy on his
legs, Cecil finds release in the grip of tides
like a woman's leg locked in contradiction

to her heart. Blood stains mark sea stones.
We travel in silence, migrating sun-bodies,
skeletal minds. Surfs hesitate to bring
the news, "Man lost at sea."

THE MARVEL OF A PERFECTLY BLUE SKY

i: *An Interruption*

Saturday before Christmas,
stuck in a line of traffic,
I became aware of
the marvel of a perfectly blue sky,
unobtrusively revealing itself, a flawless
syntax, interrupted by erratic drums.

A Jonkonnu band,
with the usual suspects:
Horse-head;
an over-age Belly Woman;
Black Devil forking his way;
children scurrying.

Man in the band insist fi block de road,
hips moving rapidly full circle, ending each
double rotation with a brap-brap, before
he drop a dutty wine no up-towner can match.
I can't help myself, a twitch escape me –
Jonkonnu gone dance-hall, Pitchy Patchy
gain wings; he can fly.

ii: *Pitchy Patchy Meets Circe on a Street in Kingston*

Pitchy Patchy chant as the band move on,
Fire fi Babylon, fire, more fire. A patch of red
sentence and composition; so much pain in purple,
bleeding into maroon, odd, nondescript, colourful
pieces stitched together, making his awkward dress
shake and shimmy like whirlwind. Whirlwind tek to sea,
and he in the street, riding the waves with horsehead,
drifting to and fro, one shore to another.
A man with much trouble, and every face was Circe,
and her voice asked, *Why suspect another trap?*
He danced, no longer coward, no longer weak;
moly from Mama's shore is magic, deep like revival.
Samples became one, mix up like pot pourri, like patwa.

He said, *When it ketch you, eye water tek you.*
But Pitchy Patchy was soon reveller again,
black monkey mask hiding years of wants.
He held out his palm, jumping and prancing,
chancing a look back, hoping to find a misstep.
He promises no miracles. His collection plate full,
he points at me, then at the crowd. I palm a fiver,
not wanting him to move on, for his back-bending
zeal was science, was sun, was moon, was salt.

iii: *Pitchy Patchy Dancing the Dance*

Pitchy danced for the lost, strip-down, flogged,
bent over in the holds of ships; overboard.
He cut new language, raw; then he step inside
of bruckings, big steps rallying against slip-ups.
Don't confuse him with the blackheart man
luring children away. Don't confuse him
with the corner don, demanding
rifle-respect in the pitch blackness of night,
though the serpent moves are much the same.
The traffic begins a slow movement.
I am closer to sky than I ever was.

iv: *Horse-head*

The line picked up speed like Horse-head,
a name deserved: "Him a de real sin-ting." He learn
to bow and scrape, turn sample into simple. But he
does not know not to show too much, too soon – like how
white people jump before the reggae-beat drop,
before the rhythm soak. Is like a secret society
move; most of us don't understand de-signs,
or know to keep out, yet they feel slighted
when we laugh. Not everything you know you show.
Horse-head never learn this lesson,
have no reserve when hungry tek him;
him sell birthright for next to nothing.
Foreigner put up fence, "Keep Out."
Horse-head never learn to play fool
fi catch wise, him head big, carrying
rivers of fear, and good for nothing.

v: *Belly Woman Contract, & Release*

The traffic still crawling, brought me in line with
a coconut tree heavy with fruit; I found myself wanting,
saw a nightingale hurrying, like he missing a friend.
I imagined that bird, wanting to be human again;
I was brought back by a shrill cry: Belly Woman
step round the corner dancing.
Oh Belly Woman, I dancing with you.
Load heavy, she hold her belly and bawl.
Is nuh little cry woman cry over man,
tears soak the land, turn flood,
is so river turn melancholy blue.
Sky see everything, call down
science fi tek blue out-a river.
So today you safe!

vi: *Suffer the Children to Come*

Children, children. "Yes Mama."
Where have you been?
"Me did out a road, Mama,
but devil out a road too."
"Devil ride Jonkonnu band
and stop by Chico shop at
the crossroads. First him
spot me, then run me down.
Never know which way to go.
Mama, him eye red like fire,
the pitchfork long, but I
make up me mind him nah ketch me.
Me tek foot and run fast fast.
Me remember the song you sing
Mama, *Hide me sweet Jesus hide me.*
Don't ever let me go. Guess what, Mama?
Is like angel tek me, carry me up in the air
push me under a bed, and so me heart
cool down, Mama. Same angel seh,
him can't ketch me again."

ZION ROSES

After Stefanie Thomas's painting titled "Zion Roses"

Oh Zion, oh Zion, carry your roses.
Oh Zion, carry your roses and come.

An early understanding of Zion, of plains
and speechless mountains, of morning

heat, of squalls and quarrels, carefully
pronounced words through closed teeth.

I can see birds hunting, a night hawk
flying, circling above green and blame,

calming storms, healing night-bodies,
lovers bending deceit like a bow.

At first light I read our vows again.
I unwrap myself into visibility.

Concerned, you offer a steady hand,
channelling gathered roses. Teacher,

you carry complex contemplations,
thorns blooming like roses in Zion.

Close, but with indifference, you
mark each step with petal-surety,

allowing me to find a way out. I follow
the beat; rain drops; a symphony of roses

lined-up like soldiers weeping. I am warrior,
I stand eloquent at the green of daybreak

balancing dawn. Light. The sun, travelling
swiftly, fires-up evening's instinct. Hunt.

Eyes sharp to spot movement. A rush
of marijuana like incense and olive oil

suffuses my nakedness; I carry roses
from a deep past steady up-mountain,

planting branches everywhere, hoping
one will catch before sunrise. Only then

will morning rays move your hand
to unlock the sweet smell you carry.

Oh Zion, oh Zion, carry your roses. Come.

NOTES

p. 7: "Bag-a-Wire – An Endangered Soul":

"goats on Redonda" alludes to the work of Shanna Challenger, an Antiguan conservationist who co-ordinated the recovery of the small, uninhabited Antiguan island of Redonda by removing feral goats and rats who had destroyed the habitat of other species.

"Bag-a-wire" is the name given to Jamaican street person, but also references the popular history of the betrayer of Marcus Garvey, once supposedly his chauffeur, condemned thereafter to life as a vagrant, as recorded in such songs as The Mighty Diamonds' "Them Never Love Poor Marcus".

"hospitable men who die in bed" alludes to Rashid Hussein, a Palestinian translator who died in bed, drunk, listening to poets; his cigarette started the fire.

p. 10: "Trombone Blues":

"bag-a-wire blues" references the poem "Bag-a-wire" in *To us all Flowers are Roses* by Lorna Goodison.

p. 16: "Passover":

"Morris's take on Pilate" refers to Mervyn Morris's collection *On Holy Week* (1976).

p. 20: "Better Strangers":

the phrase "better than strangers" alludes to Major Jackson's "The Flaneur Tends A Well-Liked Summer Cocktail", in VQR Fall, 2016.

The phrase "wild and beautiful beings" alludes to Wendell Berry's poem, "The Peace of Wild Things".

p. 23: "Set Sail":

"Keep sailing… No impurities in running water" is a Kyrgyz proverb.

p. 31: "Rundown":

The lines "Outside the kitchen window… mamas on tippy toes" echo lines from Shara McCallum's poem "What lies Beneath".

ABOUT THE AUTHOR

Winsome Monica Minott is a chartered accountant and poet. She has received two awards in the Jamaican National Book Development Council's annual literary competitions for book-length collections of her poetry.

Minott was awarded first prize in the inaugural Small Axe poetry competition. Her poems have been published in *The Caribbean Writer*, *Small Axe Caribbean Journal*, *Cultural Voice Magazine*, *SX Salon*, *Jubilation*, *Coming Up Hot* and *The Squaw Valley Review*, and more recently in *BIM* magazine. Some of her poems have been broadcast on Power 106 in Jamaica. Her debut collection, *Kumina Queen*, was published by Peepal Tree Press in 2016.

ALSO BY MONICA MINOTT

Kumina Queen
ISBN: 9781845233174; pp. 68; pub. 2016; £8.99

"This is an accomplished and pleasing first collection. Poem after poem make us sit up and think, sometimes smiling at the low-key irony, as we follow the variety of personae and topics. One of the striking areas of interest is the poet's imaginative projection of the African heritage of Jamaicans, and, in this regard, her subtle use of folk beliefs and idiom."

— Edward Baugh, author of B*lack Sand: New and Selected Poems*

"We say the best poems on the tongue contain the spiritual sounds of a culture, and here, the poetry in Monica Minott's *Kumina Queen* carries forward personal and ancestral memories line by line, song after song; here are poems that define and celebrate the contours of a life and the force of a people joyously bound together between earth and sky."

— Major Jackson, author of *Holding Company* and *Roll Deep*.

"Cultural inheritance is a recurrent feature in this rich collection. The title poem presents a persona "schooled in containment" who wishes to skip over generations keeping her in, and "dance the dance" of an earlier ancestor. Celebrating the range of Jamaican language (English, patois and various combinations), the poems explore "an ache coded / in the bloodline"; they often refer to family and female figures in African Jamaican history or legend (such as Nanny and River Mumma) who have confronted challenges. In various shapes and voices, many of the pieces also reflect cosmopolitan experience, revising classical myth ("Penelope to Calypso"), touring foreign cities (including Venice) and viewing international art. This is an impressive book."

— Mervyn Morris, author of *I been there, sort of: New and Selected Poems*